No form of art has changed more over the past few years than ballet. What seemed not long ago to be a minor form of entertainment firmly set on traditional lines has excitingly responded to new ideas, new techniques and new kinds of music and design. In doing so it has begun to win itself new audiences. This book sets out to chart and explain the changes that have taken place, to show them in their context and suggest some developments that may be still to come.

Modern Ballet is attractively and simply written by a leading ballet critic and beautifully illustrated with about 120 photographs, many of them especially taken. John Percival discusses the work of some fifty companies from the Bolshoi Ballet, the Royal Ballet and New York City Ballet to American Dance Players and Ballet Théâtre Contemporain; and among choreographers and dancers Balanchine, Yuri Grigorovich, Frederick Ashton, Martha Graham, John Cranko, Alwin Nikolais, Hans van Manen, Merce Cunningham, Fonteyn, Nureyev, Erik Bruhn.

John Percival is associate editor of the specialized monthly *Dance and Dancers* and ballet critic of *The Times*. He writes regularly for *The New York Times* on the European dance scene, is London correspondent of the *New York Dance Magazine* and one of the regular contributors to the German annual *Ballett*.

Front cover   Geoff Moore
               Remembered Motion (music Malcolm Fox) Ballet Rambert
               Nicoline Nystrom, Peter Curtis, Gayrie MacSween

Back cover   Alwin Nikolais
               Tent (music Nikolais) Alwin Nikolais Dance Theatre

Modern ballet

John Percival

Modern Ballet

Studio Vista | Dutton pictureback

General Editor David Herbert

Frontispiece
Jerome Robbins
NY Export, Opus Jazz (Robert Prince) Ballets : USA

© John Percival 1970
Designed by Gillian Greenwood
Published in Great Britain by Studio Vista Limited
Blue Star House, Highgate Hill, London N19
and in the USA by E. P. Dutton and Co. Inc.
201 Park Avenue South, New York, NY 10003
Set in 8 on 11 pt Univers 689
Made and printed in Great Britain by
Richard Clay (The Chaucer Press), Ltd, Bungay, Suffolk

SBN 289 79729 2 (paperback)
      289 79730 6 (cased)

Contents

Introduction

If this book had been written even as little as two years ago it would have been very different in its statements, assumptions and conclusions from those I must make today. The reason is that a lot of the ballet being danced now would have been completely unimaginable until this time. Not only has technique changed, but the whole approach of a young generation of choreographers, dancers and audiences has changed too.

The changes did not take place overnight, but their full strength has only lately become apparent. Starting slowly and gradually gathering force, there has been an artistic revolution in the world of ballet. Fundamentally, the difference is that what used to be mainly a pleasant but trivial entertainment has increasingly become an art form comparable with music, painting or drama in its expressiveness and ability to interest and move the spectator. Something of this quality was always present in the past (even a minor art sometimes rises above its station) and of course even now a lot of the old triviality remains. But even that is being subtly changed. What I want to do is to show the main changes in their wider social and artistic context. But to understand them one must go further back, to the situation as it was ten or fifteen years ago, and see the seeds of subsequent developments planted almost unnoticed at the time.

Jean Coralli (1779–1854) and Jules Perrot (1810–92)
Giselle (Adam) Bolshoi Ballet production by Leonid Lavrovsky
Galina Ulanova, Nikolai Fadeyechev

The background

During the early 1950s, ballet in Russia, the United States and Britain (the three main centres then as now) seemed to be developing on fairly set lines. The Russians, after a lot of experimentation in the early years of the revolution, had settled for a monumental kind of dance-drama that was easy to follow, spectacular in its effects, and had a vast popular appeal. Even the old nineteenth-century classics (still favoured for the virtuoso technique they showed off and the attractive music they used) were generally revised to emphasize their originally minimal dramatic aspects and often also to give them some uplifting content. The old romantic ballet *Giselle*, for instance—about a peasant girl who is betrayed by the man she loves, goes mad and dies, but returns as a ghost to save him—was transformed by emphasizing the hero's redemption as a result of her love.

In Britain, these same ballet classics were the mainstay of the repertory, but done straightforwardly, as nearly as possible to the intentions of the original producers—except that standards of performance, although improving all the time, reflected British ballet's lack of any long tradition. If it had not been for one outstanding ballerina, Margot Fonteyn, and two outstanding choreographers, Frederick Ashton and Antony Tudor (both of whom came to fame in the 1930s), the British companies would have had few claims to serious attention. The modern repertory, mainly small in scale, took second place to the classics in terms of audience popularity and playing time.

opposite
The Sleeping Beauty Antoinette Sibley

Marius Petipa (1818–1910)
The Sleeping Beauty (Tchaikovsky) Royal Ballet production by Peter Wright and Frederick Ashton

Things were different in America, thanks to another long-established choreographer, the emigré Russian George Balanchine, who directed a series of companies from The American Ballet in the 1930s until New York City Ballet (founded 1948). Balanchine effectively dominated the American scene; only one American-born choreographer, Jerome Robbins, showed promise of real stature. The main rivals to New York City Ballet were primarily imitations of the earlier Ballets Russes tradition, based on a combination of the classics (usually in chopped-down digest versions) and works from, or in the tradition of, the Diaghilev company which popularized ballet in the west during the first third of this century. Curiously, British ballet in its formative years showed far less direct Diaghilev influence, going instead to the fountainhead of the Russian imperial tradition from which Diaghilev himself sprang.

What needs to be remembered is that ballet in Britain and America was still very young. In both countries it had effectively started during the 1930s, enlarged and matured during the 1940s and was in a period of consolidation during the 1950s. There had been a limited amount of cross-fertilization, notably when Tudor, one of the early leaders of British ballet, went to live and work in America. American Ballet Theatre and New York City Ballet both crossed the Atlantic to play several seasons in Europe during the decade 1946–56, and from 1949 onwards the Sadler's Wells Ballet (later the Royal Ballet) made regular trips from Britain to North America.

The great leap forward began at Covent Garden on 3 October 1956 when the Bolshoi Ballet from Moscow opened its first season in the west with Galina Ulanova dancing in *Romeo and Juliet*. Suddenly British and American ballet were faced with a new standard of comparison. Not only was Ulanova generally recognized as the greatest dancer of her day, but the qualities she possessed were found in some degree all through the company, and the ballet itself took the old style of dance-drama to its furthest peak. An intensely dramatic style of dancing, absolute wholeheartedness of presentation, large-scale effects, male dancers who swept and soared across the stage in an unrivalled way, and partnering which deliberately introduced acrobatic tricks to extend the expressive range of the dance—all these hit an audience which had never seen anything of the sort before. Subsequent visits to

Leonid Lavrovsky (1905–67)
Romeo and Juliet (Prokofiev) **The** Bolshoi Ballet
Sergei Koren, Alexei Yermolaev

Britain and America by the same company and the Kirov Ballet from Leningrad—a slightly more elegant and reticent, even more 'aristocratic' company, but still in the same tradition—confirmed the impression of that first season. The local companies had to respond.

The first result was direct imitation. The best of the younger dancers first managed to emulate some of the Russian tricks, especially in partnering, then others simply had to follow. One easily measurable indication of this effect is the way ballerinas, instead of merely being lifted to shoulder height by their partners, are nowadays customarily held high above the man's head at the full stretch of his arms, or even on one arm. This style was introduced into Soviet ballet by the choreographer Feodor Lopukhov and attacked by one critic as 'more gynaecology than ballet' but its greater effectiveness has now won it universal acceptance.

Tricks came first; the use of this extended technique for dramatic purposes followed as the younger choreographers especially tried to bring into their work something of the seriousness and humanity they saw in the best of the Russian ballets. And while the west learned breadth of movement and depth of content from the Russians, these in turn tried to adapt for their own purposes qualities they found in the west, in particular the greater use of dance rather than acting to tell their stories.

While these waves of influence flowed east and west, another current began to make itself felt. The first lappings of it were apparent even earlier, when the American modern dancer Martha Graham brought her company for a London season in 1954. But although a few people greatly admired her work, audiences were tiny. The same was true for a later tour by a company headed by José Limón with the noted teacher, choreographer and theorist Doris Humphrey as artistic director. Not until 1963, when Graham enjoyed an unprecedented success at the Edinburgh Festival, did this tide really gather strength.

That is the background to the changes that have been taking place in ballet. Some of the changes flow directly from these events; others were influenced by developments in the other arts or in society generally; some were brought about by a single gifted individual.

Anna-Marie Holmes and David Holmes
Canadian dancers trained at the Kirov School, Leningrad

A new heart for ballet

The importance one creative and strong-minded person can have is strikingly shown by the way one major company alone has remained remarkably unaffected by the changes taking place all around it. This is New York City Ballet, and the explanation is the almost autocratic power exercised by the company's chief choreographer and artistic director, George Balanchine. Born in St Petersburg, educated at the Russian imperial school of ballet there, a choreographer (and a revolutionary one, too) almost from the beginning of his career, Balanchine left Russia in 1924, soon made a name, and was invited in 1933 to organize a school and company of American ballet from which, after various vicissitudes, his present company developed.

In sheer quantity Balanchine completely dominates the ballet scene throughout America and western Europe. More than forty of his works are currently in the New York City Ballet repertory, besides a great many more which have been given in the past and dropped. Others are danced by major companies in at least a dozen European cities, while several of the smaller American and Canadian companies rely on his ballets as the basis of their repertory. No other choreographer has ever had so many ballets performed so widely or so often.

Nobody reaches such a position without remarkable gifts. Balanchine can turn his hand to almost any kind of ballet (his favourite comparisons to explain his work are with the craftsmanship of a carpenter or the skill of a chef, both making what the customer wants) but he has little interest in using dancing to tell a story. The beginnings of his greatness can be traced to his oldest surviving work, *Apollo* (created in 1928) in which the simplicity and muscular strength of Stravinsky's music encouraged the young choreographer to aim at similar qualities. The ballet had an austere beauty that has proved timeless. In it, the strict academic technique of the classical tradition was partly remoulded to suit the theme, the music and the dancers for whom it was created.

That is fundamentally the way Balanchine has worked ever since. Nowadays most of his works fall into one or other of two categories. On the one hand he uses the old virtuoso classical technique for ballets either of sheer brilliant dance display or of a

George Balanchine (b. 1904)
Apollo (Stravinsky) New York City Ballet
Patricia Wilde, Jacques d'Amboise, Jillana

mistily romantic mood. These range in their musical basis from the rum-ti-tum style of the nineteenth-century classics (Glinka or Drigo) through Tchaikovsky, Glazunov and Delibes to Bizet and Fauré, Brahms and Ravel, or even Mozart and Stravinsky. Stravinsky's recent music, however, has often served Balanchine for his other favourite form, in which the old open, straightforward bravura style is changed into a very personal manner with turned-in feet, bent arms and legs, unexpected quirks, twists and bends of

George Balanchine
Western Symphony (Hershy Kay) New York City Ballet
Nicholas Magallanes, Melissa Hayden

George Balanchine
Serenade (Tchaikovsky) New York City Ballet
Nicholas Magallanes, Patricia Wilde

George Balanchine
Night Shadow (music by Vittorio Rieti on themes by Bellini) London's Festival Ballet
John Gilpin, Galina Samtsova

George Balanchine
The Prodigal Son (Prokofiev) New York City Ballet
Edward Villella, Patricia Neary

the body, and rhythms that sink or rise in a surprising way. First seen to illustrate the theme of *The Four Temperaments* (to commissioned music by Hindemith in 1946), this style has subsequently been turned by Balanchine into a way of setting abstract dances to contemporary music. *Agon* (Stravinsky, 1957) is the most widely known example—tense, sinewy, brief and compressed, with an unexpected underlying humour—but Webern, Charles Ives, Yannis Xenakis and others have been treated in this way.

George Balanchine
The Four Temperaments (Hindemith) New York City Ballet
Arthur Mitchell

What makes Balanchine's work outstanding is, first, his flair for making his dancers look attractive in movement, and secondly his unsurpassed understanding of music as a basis for the dance. These qualities, sustained over the years, give his company its homogeneity. Certainly he himself has developed (lately, for instance, he has turned increasingly to a genre he formerly avoided, the long spectacular ballet occupying a full evening on its own) but all his developments spring logically from within.

George Balanchine
Agon (Stravinsky) New York City Ballet
Arthur Mitchell, Allegra Kent

It was New York City Ballet in 1959 that partly anticipated, though apparently without realizing the implications, one of the trends of the following decade. Deciding to present a ballet to all the works written by Webern for orchestra alone, Balanchine and his general director Lincoln Kirstein invited Martha Graham to undertake part of the choreography and bring her own company as guest artists. The resulting ballet, *Episodes*, as its name implies was not a real collaboration. Graham's part was a story ballet about Mary Queen of Scots. Balanchine produced a series of exciting but austere dances in his inverted-classic manner, and incidentally introduced another modern dancer, Paul Taylor, to dance a solo specially created by Balanchine in something close to Taylor's own personal style. Subsequently, *Episodes* remained in the repertory without the modern dance sections, but symbolically this occasion marked the coming together of traditions which had been regarded as mutually incompatible.

opposite
Episodes Anthony Blum, Mimi Paul

George Balanchine
Episodes (Webern) New York City Ballet

At this time, however, the main influence on classical ballet was still the cross-fertilization of the Soviet and western schools. Balanchine may have been little affected, or even not at all; others were anxious to learn all they could. With the Royal Ballet, for instance, John Cranko's *The Prince of the Pagodas,* produced only three months after the Bolshoi season at Covent Garden, was already full of the high Russian-style lifts. Cranko was also one of the choreographers who went on to a deeper understanding of the underlying approach of the Russians. His *Antigone* (1959) showed no direct stylistic influence of the Russians; in fact the choreographer most influencing him at the time was Jerome Robbins. But the content of *Antigone,* an impassioned plea for an individual stand against war, reflected the dissatisfaction with trivialities which followed exposure to the seriousness and dramatic intensity of the Bolshoi Ballet.

John Cranko (b. 1927)
The Prince of the Pagodas (Britten) The Royal Ballet
David Blair, Svetlana Beriosova

John Cranko
Antigone (Theodorakis) The Royal Ballet

Cranko's colleague Kenneth MacMillan, also at that time a choreographer with the Royal Ballet, was similarly affected and turned from the artificial drama of his early ballets to subjects like *The Invitation* in which he tried to show credible characters in an explosive situation : a boy and girl involved sexually (and for the girl disastrously) with an older couple.

This sort of indirect response to the Russian stimulus was matched elsewhere by a more direct influence. The Soviet choreographer Vladimir Bourmeister, who had been in charge of the Stanislavsky Ballet in Moscow, was invited to stage his famous production of *Swan Lake* (with its attempt to adapt the story as a clearer struggle between good and evil, and a spectacular last scene which incorporates an illusion of actually flooding the stage) for the leading French company at the Paris Opéra in 1960. The following year he actually created an entirely

Kenneth MacMillan (b. 1930)
The Invitation (Matyas Seiber) The Royal Ballet
Marilyn Trounson

new three-act ballet, *The Snow Maiden*, for London's Festival Ballet. Based on a Russian folk tale, using Russian folk dance and Soviet-style classicism as the basis of its choreography, this was an ambitious and at least partly successful attempt at importing the Russian style complete. (Later, Bourmeister revived the ballet in Moscow.)

Another Russian-born choreographer, Vaslav Orlikovsky, already working in Germany and Switzerland, began to become more prominent about this time. He too staged several works for Festival Ballet (including a full-evening production of *Peer Gynt* which proved very popular for a while) and a lavish *Cinderella* for a specially formed company in Paris. Later he became director of ballet at the Vienna State Opera.

The greatest Russian influence on the west, however, was in the approach to producing the standard classics. Except in Denmark (which maintained its own nineteenth-century tradition with the ballets of August Bournonville) and Russia (where a larger number of Petipa's old productions survived either complete or in fragmentary form), companies wanting a traditional basis for their work relied almost entirely on five ballets, all of them either originally staged or at least substantially revised by Marius Petipa or his assistant Lev Ivanov in St Petersburg for the Russian imperial ballet in the latter part of the nineteenth century. These five ballets (*Giselle* and *Coppélia*, both adapted from French originals, and the Tchaikovsky ballets *Swan Lake*, *The Sleeping Beauty* and *The Nutcracker*) dominated the international repertory from San Francisco to Vladivostok, from Stockholm to Cape Town, to an extent explained by, but out of all proportion to, their enduring merits of plot, music and dance. Once the Stanislavsky *Swan Lake*, the Bolshoi *Giselle* and the Kirov *Sleeping Beauty* had been seen in the west, ideas about the most suitable stylistic and dramatic approach to these works began to change. Soviet choreographers and producers were invited to stage them in many European and North American cities, and western producers began to rethink their own versions. Sometimes the ideas were only half digested and the results disastrous, as with the Royal Ballet's 1963 production of *Swan Lake*, which threw away some of the best of the traditional dances and introduced confused and unnecessary additions to the plot. (A tacit admission of this production's deficiencies came with the changes soon introduced, bringing it back towards a more traditional form; and also the mounting of a completely different version for the Royal Ballet's touring company.) On the other hand, a whole new generation of skilled producers began to emerge, notable among them being Peter Wright, with a marvellously clear and intelligent interpretation of

Vladimir Bourmeister (b. 1904)
The Snow Maiden (Tchaikovsky) London's Festival Ballet
Oleg Briansky, Marilyn Burr

Giselle in Stuttgart and later in London; David Blair, whose versions of *Swan Lake* and *The Sleeping Beauty* were given by American Ballet Theatre and the Atlanta Ballet; and Ben Stevenson with a production of *The Sleeping Beauty* for London's Festival Ballet.

Yet the traffic in ideas between Russia and the west was not only one way. Inside Russia the old monumental, solidly plotted

Marius Petipa
The Sleeping Beauty (Tchaikovsky) Festival Ballet production by Ben Stevenson
John Gilpin, Noëlla Pontois

kind of production continued. An example of its merits was the *Othello* mounted by Vakhtang Chabukiani in 1957 for the company he directs at Tbilisi. An uneven work, it was distinguished by the heroic ambitiousness of its theme and its striking incarnation of the leading characters, especially Othello himself as a figure bold, impetuous and free from all contriving, and a surly disdainful Iago, outwardly bluff but revealed in his dances to be as

Vakhtang Chabukiani (b. 1910)
Othello (Alexei Machavariani) Georgian State Ballet, Tbilisi
Bekar Monavardissashvili, Zurab Kikaleishvili

insinuating as a snake and as dangerous as a hawk. About the same time, however, the young choreographer Yuri Grigorovich staged a new version of Prokofiev's *The Stone Flower* which began a fresh tendency in Soviet ballet. *The Stone Flower* had previously been unsuccessful in a traditional production by Leonid Lavrovsky (the creator of *Romeo and Juliet*). Grigorovich reconceived it as a series of dance episodes telling the story in dance terms without old-fashioned mime. He rearranged the musical sequence as well as inventing new choreography, and in this form the ballet was successful enough to be staged, after its Kirov première, also at the Bolshoi and in Novosibirsk.

Grigorovich's inspiration for this approach came primarily from the veteran (and at that time partly discredited) choreographer Feodor Lopukhov, who had been responsible in the early days of the Russian revolution both for preserving the classical heritage, which he regarded as a necessary basis for any experiment, and also for many innovations. Lopukhov was one of several people prominent in Soviet ballet in the mid-1950s (the choreographer and folk-dance group director Igor Moiseyev was another, and Ulanova a third) who were dissatisfied with the heavy emphasis on the content of ballet and wanted greater concern for form on the one hand and expressiveness on the other. These thoughts were emphasized soon afterwards when Grigorovich and other young Russian artists had their first chance to see a ballet by Balanchine, his brilliant display piece to Bizet's Symphony in C, performed by the Paris Opéra Ballet as *Le Palais de Crystal* and included on the Russian tour they made. This was much admired, and so were other works (especially *Episodes*, surprisingly enough, since it was unlike anything the Russians had seen before) when New York City Ballet went to Moscow and Leningrad in 1962. Nobody at the time actually copied Balanchine's completely plotless style, but Asaf Messerer's *School of Ballet* came close to it. This virtuoso display piece, based on a ballet class, was a special case, because it was created specifically at the suggestion of the American impresario S. Hurok and actually first performed during an American tour in 1962. The same year, however, also saw the production of Kasyan Goleizovsky's *Scriabiniana*, an unrelated suite of dances to Scriabin music. The previous year Igor Belsky had staged his *Leningrad Symphony* in which the theme of the German invasion and siege was treated in almost abstract dance terms. In Russia as in the west, things were changing.

Meanwhile, the first stirrings of other trends began to be felt. In Paris in 1958 was given an abysmally bad ballet, *Le Rendezvous Manqué* (also given in Britain and the United States as *Broken Date*). This would not deserve even passing mention here if it were not symptomatic of better things to come. One or two good dancers and a reputable choreographer (John Taras, subsequently Balanchine's chief assistant) could not disguise the tawdry conception of the work by some celebrities previously unconnected with ballet, Françoise Sagan as author and Roger Vadim as producer. Yet the work was an innovation in one respect—an attempt to make ballet appeal to a popular audience. In London, for instance, it played in a large theatre normally used as a cinema. Roland Petit's *Cyrano de Bergerac*, also given a commercial run in Paris and London, was a similar attempt soon afterwards at putting on a popular show in the form of ballet; later this formed part of Petit's film *Black Tights* which, with commentary by Maurice Chevalier, was clearly aimed at a general audience.

Another choreographer who has attempted something similar was beginning to make a name about this same time. This was Maurice Béjart, whose *Orphée* in 1958 was an early example of the mixture of dance, speech, electronic music and universal myth which has since become the basis of his most popular works. Béjart has shown enormous daring and enterprise. After running his own small company from 1954, he staged Stravinsky's *Rite of*

Igor Belsky (b. 1925)
Leningrad Symphony (Shostakovich) The Kirov Ballet

Maurice Béjart (b. 1928)
Ninth Symphony (Beethoven) Ballet du XXe Siècle, Brussels

Spring for the Royal Theatre in Brussels at the end of 1959 and on
the strength of its public success became director of the resident
company there, renaming it Le Ballet du XXe Siècle (Twentieth
Century Ballet). The grandiose but challenging title is characteristic. Béjart pioneered gigantic spectacles to be given in vast
auditoria like the Royal Circus in Brussels, the Palais des Sports in
Paris and the Murrayfield Ice Stadium, Edinburgh. One such was
Ninth Symphony, in which he used Beethoven's music. Wagner
also served him for a full evening's programme, and Berlioz
(*Romeo and Juliet*) for another. Both in Belgium and in France
(where he has staged several works for the Opéra, and where his
own company appears frequently) Béjart has found a huge
following. His work has severe limitations. In particular, his skill
as an arranger of dance lags well behind his daring as a producer,
and having chosen a revolutionary theme he will often try to
sustain any flagging interest by the inclusion of completely conventional solos. But if his choreography is sometimes banal, his
dancers are good, and certainly the provocative subjects and
iconoclastic treatment find a response among young people who
would never be interested by more traditional styles.

Jerome Robbins (b. 1918)
NY Export, Opus Jazz (Robert Prince) Ballets: USA

That it is possible to appeal to wide audiences without resorting to sensationalism is shown by the career of Jerome Robbins. Right from the start he worked in the commercial theatre as well as ballet; his first ballet, *Fancy Free*, formed the basis of the musical *On the Town*. Later, after working with both American Ballet Theatre and New York City Ballet, Robbins conceived and produced *West Side Story*, which enjoyed equal (and equally widespread) success in both stage and screen versions.

In 1958 Robbins started his own company, Ballets: USA, originally for appearances at the first Festival of Two Worlds organized by Gian-Carlo Menotti at Spoleto and in the US Pavilion at the Brussels World Fair. A further tour of Europe and a New York season followed, but thereafter the company appeared only sporadically, with tours in 1959 and 1961 and a single performance at the White House (its last engagement) in 1962. For this company Robbins created three major works—*Moves*, described as 'a ballet in silence about relationships', and two with symphonic jazz scores by Robert Prince: *NY Export, Opus Jazz* and *Events*. In these works, Robbins used his dancers in a jazz-flavoured version of classical dancing which was revolutionary in catching the coolness and detachment as well as the energy of American life. More important than the fact that they wore sneakers and jeans instead of the soft slippers and tights of traditional ballet was the feeling they conveyed of a specifically American and specifically contemporary way of life. The company's repertory also included one of the funniest ballets in years, *The Concert*, to music by Chopin; Robbins is one of the few choreographers who can successfully be funny just as well as he can be serious. Robbins' long estrangement from ballet after the disbanding of his company was a source of bitter regret; luckily when he returned it was (as we shall see) with no loss of impact or originality.

The impact of Robbins on Europe was a foretaste of the sort of effect American modern dance was to have not much later—but before this, two more influences from the old world were to make themselves strongly felt. One began with the startling defection from the Kirov Ballet, just as the company was leaving Paris after a season there in 1961, of a young dancer of exceptional promise. Thus Rudolf Nureyev started his career in the west by hitting the headlines from which he has seldom been absent since. After appearing with the Grand Ballet du Marquis de Cuevas and in a small concert group as partner to the American ballerina Rosella Hightower, Nureyev in 1962 played his first guest season with the Royal Ballet in London and has been associated with that company ever since, although he has also made guest appearances all over the world, besides staging ballets in London, Vienna, Milan, Stockholm and elsewhere.

This was the first time a western company had experienced the presence of a Soviet dancer (and an exceptional one at that) actually alternating roles with its own male dancers, although the Royal Ballet did have a Soviet ballerina, Violetta Elvin (Prokhorova) for ten years from 1946. The effect on British male dancers was immediately traumatic but in the long run beneficial. If they were not to suffer in the comparison they simply had to learn, for instance, to jump higher than they had in the past. Luckily there were some respects in which Nureyev himself, for all his bravura and charismatic personality, was by no means impeccable (his strength as a partner, in particular, was limited) and this prevented dancers from being too disheartened even to try to compete. Also, especially once he began producing ballets for the company, starting with a revival of a scene from Petipa's *Bayaderka*, he revealed himself as a good teacher.

One unforeseeable result of Nureyev's advent was a new lease of life for Margot Fonteyn, who at the time of his arrival was showing the first signs that her long supremacy among ballerinas (since Ulanova's retirement, Fonteyn and Maya Plisetskaya of the

Frederick Ashton (b. 1906)
Marguerite and Armand (Liszt) The Royal Ballet
Margot Fonteyn

Bolshoi shone above all rivals) might be approaching its end. Her technique had begun to slip; more important, her confidence also looked like going. Nureyev changed all that. Dancing with him, responding to his highly charged stage presence, she found a dramatic power which had previously eluded her. In place of the formerly rather reserved, carefully balanced dancer emerged a woman who threw herself impetuously into her roles. The old Fonteyn could never have impersonated successfully the impassioned courtesan heroine of Frederick Ashton's *Marguerite and Armand*, although equally the Fonteyn of the later years could no longer dance a lyrical role like the one created for her (by the same choreographer) in *Symphonic Variations*, which therefore passed to a younger generation of dancers.

opposite, Marguerite and Armand Margot Fonteyn, Rudolf Nureyev

Frederick Ashton
Symphonic Variations (César Franck) The Royal Ballet
Anthony Dowell, Antoinette Sibley

Nureyev was not the only famous male dancer to appear as guest star at Covent Garden in 1962. Erik Bruhn was invited too, not only to dance (his Apollonian style making a complete contrast with Nureyev's Dionysiac qualities) but also to stage two short pieces by Bournonville. Danish by birth and training, Bruhn was brought up in the light, crisp, easy but exact style which Bournonville learned in Paris early in the nineteenth century and fostered in Copenhagen during his career as leader of the Royal Danish Ballet for nearly fifty years. During that time he built up a

August Bournonville (1805–97)
Napoli (Paulli, Helsted, Gade and Lumbye) Royal Danish Ballet
Niels Kehlet, Solveig Østergaard, Inge Sand

repertory of masterpieces which remained almost unknown outside Denmark but were preserved there all the more lovingly because no other choreographer of anything approaching Bournonville's stature arose within the Danish ballet. Bournonville had always hoped for fame abroad but never found it. Ironically, three-quarters of a century after his death, he won a posthumous international reputation during the 1950s and early 1960s when his version of *La Sylphide* and extracts from his long ballets *Napoli* and *The Conservatoire*, together with some shorter

Napoli Niels Kehlet

divertissements, were mounted for companies all over Europe and America by Harald Lander (former ballet director in Copenhagen), Bruhn and others. With these, and with Nureyev's classic revivals also (*Raymonda* and *Don Quixote* as well as *Bayaderka*) the choice of standard classics became much less restricted than in the past.

At the same time, various people working within the classical ballet tradition were trying to extend the scope of that tradition. They tended to work mainly in small companies: the Robert Joffrey Ballet in America and Ballet Rambert in Britain, for

August Bournonville
The Conservatoire (Paulli) Royal Danish Ballet

Peter Darrell (b. 1929)
The Prisoners (Bartók) Western Theatre Ballet
Simon Mottram, Elaine McDonald, Peter Cazalet

instance (both of which were transformed by subsequent developments and are therefore discussed later), and another British
company, Western Theatre Ballet. This was formed in 1957 in an
attempt to give Britain a regional company, based on Bristol. Lack
of local support soon forced the company on to the usual touring
circuit, but it stayed faithful to another of its original intentions,
of using the classical ballet technique in a more dramatic and
more entertaining way. Peter Darrell, the company's resident
choreographer and artistic director, achieved this in the very first
programme they gave, with his ballet *The Prisoners* about a gaol
break followed by murder which leads one of the escapers to find
he has only exchanged one prison for another at the hands of a

woman who shelters and dominates him. Darrell had a flair for comedy also (usually of a rather dark kind) which kept the company going through some sticky patches, but his *Wedding Present*, about a marriage ruined when the wife finds her husband had a homosexual lover, proved one of the few ballets to achieve true tragedy rather than pathos. *Mods and Rockers*, based on pop

on pages 56 *and* 57
Peter Darrell
Sun into Darkness (Malcolm Williamson) Western Theatre Ballet
Simon Mottram, Donna Day Washington

opposite
The Wedding Present Brenda Last, Laverne Meyer

Peter Darrell
The Wedding Present (Bartók) Western Theatre Ballet

dances and set to Beatles music just as they were about to change from children's idols to international figures, gave the company wide popularity. In 1966, taking advantage of facilities provided by a link with Sadler's Wells Opera, Darrell created the first full-evening British ballet with a contemporary setting, *Sun into Darkness*. Based on the theme of a village carnival turning almost accidentally into an orgiastic ritual murder, this ballet introduced

opposite, Mods and Rockers

Peter Darrell
Mods and Rockers (John Lennon, Paul McCartney and George Harrison)
Western Theatre Ballet

some new ideas in presentation. Not only was a playwright, David Rudkin, responsible for the plot, but a theatrical and operatic producer, Colin Graham, was involved jointly with the choreographer at all stages of preparation. This innovation, repeated with success for further new works and revivals, helped stimulate Western Theatre Ballet's most impressive achievement, the dramatic flair and feeling for ensemble playing which its dancers developed. This quality was particularly apparent when Jack Carter, an experienced and versatile choreographer, was invited to work with the company, and inspired him to possibly his most original and sensitively developed work, *Cage of God*, which interpreted the fall of man as a rather sinister practical joke by the Almighty.

But Western Theatre Ballet's achievements were won against the tide, which by the 1960s was beginning to flow fast towards a different kind of dancing which questioned the supremacy of, or even the need for, the long-established classical tradition.

Jack Carter (b. 1924)
Cage of God (Alan Rawsthorne) Western Theatre Ballet

A new way of dancing

The name 'modern dance' is awkward and vague but I must use it for want of any better to describe the kind of dancing evolved in this century as an alternative to classical ballet. The word modern grows more questionable all the time in this context, since the movement can be traced back certainly as far as Isadora Duncan and other equally revolutionary but less famous dancers who flourished at the beginning of the century. Duncan's free style (which, judging from contemporary accounts and pictures, must have been far more varied and strong than one would guess from the Vanessa Redgrave movie) was based partly on imagined Greek antiquity and served more as inspiration than model for those who came after. There was also a more tense style developed in Germany which flourished in the 1920s and 1930s but has virtually died out since. For practical purposes, most 'modern dance' today springs from pupils of one of Duncan's American contemporaries, Ruth St Denis, and her husband Ted Shawn. Their Denishawn School flourished, first in Los Angeles and later in New York, for about fifteen years from 1915, and among the most prominent pupils were the leaders of the next generation of modern dancers, Martha Graham, Doris Humphrey and Charles Weidman, all of whom formed their artistic policies by reaction against the simple movement interpretations they had been taught.

In their generation, modern dance was primarily a solo art. In contrast to classical ballet, where the dancer must acquire the accepted technique and style, modern dance tried to evolve techniques and styles to fit the individual dancers. What makes Martha Graham pre-eminent is the quality of her own gifts as dancer and choreographer, but what makes her so influential is the fact that from the experience she gained over the years she evolved a technique that could be codified and taught by progressive daily exercises in the same way as classical ballet. It is based on a simple idea, the tension between opposites: balance and falling, or the contractions and stretching involved in breathing. To teach this comprehensive and consistent method she had evolved, Graham established a school in New York. The economic

Martha Graham (b. 1893)
Night Journey (William Schuman) Martha Graham Dance Company
Erick Hawkins, Graham

circumstances of modern dance were such that Graham and the company she formed could usually perform for only a few consecutive weeks at a time. Between seasons, she and her leading dancers supported themselves by teaching at the school; several of the dancers also organized their own performing groups at intervals to dance their own choreography.

Martha Graham
Alcestis (Vivian Fine) Martha Graham Dance Company
Graham, Bertram Ross

Martha Graham
Cave of the Heart (Samuel Barber) Martha Graham Dance Company
Graham

Graham's work developed from an attempt to give physical expression to inward feelings. This is true even of the richly inventive series of almost abstract group ballets she has created for the dancers of her company. *Diversion of Angels*, for instance, carries definite moods and makes much of contrasts between the personalities of its soloists, such as one girl lyrically ecstatic and another gravely serene. In *Acrobats of God* she used one of her own classes as the basis for a delicately funny work with the dancers toiling away, herself wandering among them in search of inspiration, and her rehearsal assistant literally cracking a whip

opposite, Dark Meadow

Martha Graham
Dark Meadow (Carlos Chavez) Martha Graham Dance Company
Matt Turney

over everybody. Ballets of this sort continue the rituals which have always formed part of her creative work. Recently, leaving aside the specifically American subjects (like *Appalachian Spring* or the Emily Dickinson ballet *Letter to the World*) she often adopted earlier, most of her other works have taken the form of an analysis of the thoughts, fears and dreams of a mythological, historical or biblical person. These dance dramas were usually built around her own gifts as a performer, although with advancing years (few people realized that Graham was already over sixty by the time of her first London season in 1954) she has tended to make the central role less arduous. Typical Graham subjects were the Freudian *Night Journey* (the Oedipus legend with Jocasta as the central character), a startlingly uninhibited *Phaedra*, the biblical

Martha Graham
Clytemnestra (Halim El-Dabh) Martha Graham Dance Company
Graham

Martha Graham
Seraphic Dialogue (Norman Dello Joio) Martha Graham Dance Company

Legend of Judith with its horrifying picture of Holofernes' head rolling in a blanket and the headless corpse returning to haunt her dreams, and *Errand into the Maze* where the Minotaur legend became the basis of an exploration of deep-seated human fears. But she also produced *Seraphic Dialogue*, based on various aspects of Joan of Arc (as Maid, Warrior and Martyr, finally becoming St Joan) which, although some passages reflected terror or frenzy, was fundamentally joyous in its mood. Her largest-scale work, *Clytemnestra*, is a three-act exploration of the whole Theban myth, as gripping as it is ambitious.

Merce Cunningham
Variations V (John Cage) Merce Cunningham Dance Company

Most of the leaders of the next generation of American modern dancers graduated through Graham's company. Erick Hawkins, for many years her leading male dancer, left to form his own group for avant-garde experiments. In this respect he was rather eclipsed by another former Graham soloist, Merce Cunningham, who has had his own company since 1952. His close association with the composer John Cage and, for a while, with the painter Robert Rauschenberg (both of them famous if controversial figures in their own spheres) ensured Cunningham a certain notoriety, but he had genuine gifts of his own to deserve attention.

Variations V Barbara Lloyd, Cunningham

Cage, with his theories of composition involving some elements left to chance, had an important influence on Cunningham's choreography, In *Variations V,* Cage's music was actually controlled in performance by the dancers' movements haphazardly affecting photo-electric cells arranged around the stage. Similarly, Cunningham introduced chance into some of his dances, either as an element in composition or even (although only in a few works) allowing the dancers a measure of choice during performance, so that a given work was never twice exactly alike. This happened for instance in *Story* (so called, apparently, because there was no story to it) where the pre-determined episodes could take a different shape and even follow a different order, and where Rauschenberg improvised scenery during the action—even, during one run of performances in London, painting a picture on stage, a bit more each night. The effect was unpredictable : sometimes the ballet could completely misfire, but other times it might take on a tension and dramatic effect from unplanned qualities that might never have been found consciously. It could also, incidentally, be funny one night and frightening another.

The use of chance attracted generally more attention than the seriously composed elements in Cunningham's work. But audiences attracted by his notoriety discovered a choreographer with the rare virtue of taking nothing for granted. His ballets could be outrageously funny (like *Antic Meet,* in one episode of which he became involved with a sweater that had four arms but no neck), coolly beautiful (*Nocturnes,* for instance, to Satie music) or inexplicably but terrifyingly tragic, like *Winterbranch* with its images of bodies falling, crawling or scurrying in darkness lit by flashing beams. Objects took great importance in his work ; so did light and darkness, silence and almost unbearable noise.

Merce Cunningham
Winterbranch (LaMonte Young) Merce Cunningham Dance Company
Carolyn Brown

A complete contrast was Paul Taylor, who also graduated from being a Graham soloist to running his own company. What particularly endeared his work to audiences was the bubbling humour of ballets like *Piece Period* (a kind of period piece in reverse, parodying various affectations of style) and *3 Epitaphs* (an almost surrealistic joke setting vaudeville-style dances to music by the Laneville-Johnson Union Brass Band with the

Paul Taylor (b. 1930)
Aureole (Handel) Royal Danish Ballet

dancers in ghoulishly black costumes by Rauschenberg) ; also the pure lyrical style of his *Aureole* to Handel music. Yet Taylor also created in a variety of styles. *Party Mix* was a sardonic look at social life, not unlike an updated version of Bronislava Nijinska's famous ballet *Les Biches* from the 1920s; and in *Scudorama* Taylor deliberately set out to evoke a mood of nausea and disgust.

Aureole

One of the few major figures not associated with Graham was José Limón, a pupil of Graham's contemporary Doris Humphrey. After her own performing career ended, Humphrey became artistic director of Limón's company (until her death in 1958) and with Limón its chief choreographer. This company's characteristic style was a more sculptural one, leading to a heroic and dignified but still expressive manner in works like *Lament for Ignacio Sanchez Mejias,* based by Humphrey on Lorca's poem about the death of a bullfighter, or Limón's *The Moor's Pavane*, a formal dance for four people with the passions of Othello, Iago, Desdemona and Emilia burning just below the surface. Humphrey also founded a modern dance performing company for students of the Juilliard School in New York, and Limón was associated with attempts in the mid-1960s to establish a permanent repertory company for modern dance in America, presenting the works of many choreographers.

This was an unusual idea in the modern dance world, although the usual practice in ballet companies. One modern dance company that successfully accomplished it, however, was that of Alvin Ailey. Besides his own works, among which the most notable was the beautiful and moving suite of dances to spirituals, *Revelations*, Ailey presented dances by his teacher Lester Horton (a cramped but impressive talent), Anna Sokolow and Talley Beatty. Sokolow (who also has her own company) staged her sombre *Rooms* for Ailey, a biting study of loneliness, and Beatty contributed extracts from his long work *Come and get the beauty of it hot*, in which outwardly smooth dance passages revealed a hidden temper, and also the explosively dramatic *Road of the 'Phoebe Snow'* based on ghetto life behind the railway tracks with transitory affection, sexual violence and jealousy exacerbated by poverty.

It is a curious thing that these and other American modern dance companies enjoyed only limited (although enthusiastic) support in their own country until they first conquered the resistance of the London audience which had previously had no time at all for modern dance (except earlier in the rather different German tradition represented by Kurt Jooss' company, which found a

William Louther
Soloist of Alvin Ailey, Martha Graham and London Contemporary Dance Companies

home in England when Jooss went into exile from Hitler's regime).
Visits to London by Graham and Limón in the 1950s excited a few,
but they played to nearly empty houses. In 1963 a fanatical admirer
of Graham, Robin Howard, raised guarantees to bring her company to the Edinburgh Festival and for a season in London. Taste
had meanwhile changed and she enjoyed a wild success, not
only with the general public but with dancers, artists and theatre
people on whom her innovations exerted an influence such as she
had never known before.

The impact of Graham's London season was consolidated
when, during the following year, no fewer than three other companies (Cunningham, Ailey and Taylor) followed her there. These
companies between them gave a fair cross-section of the activities

London School of Contemporary Dance
Martha Graham class

of the American modern dance scene. What they demonstrated was a way of dancing concerned to show off the individual qualities of the dancers rather than mould them to a pre-determined style. They were also more likely than classical ballet to find themes and subjects for their works which were of direct human appeal, and to be related in their music and design to current developments in the other arts. For these reasons they began to attract the enthusiasm of a new young audience. To meet this enthusiasm, Robin Howard launched an appeal (and himself contributed substantial funds) to set up a school of contemporary dance in London, with the eventual aim of forming a British modern dance company. Martha Graham acted as artistic adviser to the school and Robert Cohan, one of her principal dancers, was appointed artistic director.

The companies which had caused all the excitement in London themselves benefited in an unexpected way from their visits. Hitherto, their American audiences had been a limited minority; they played in small off-Broadway theatres for limited engagements and kept going mainly by tours of the 'college circuit' of universities throughout the United States, including those with an active theatre arts faculty. The general enthusiasm the companies aroused in London (the fact, for instance, that after a week of packed audiences at Sadler's Wells, Cunningham was able to transfer to the central Phoenix Theatre—usually a commercial theatre—for a further three weeks) enormously increased their standing at home and led eventually to a more secure basis for their work.

Meanwhile, another European company which was using the modern dance influence in a different way began to make itself known abroad. This was Netherlands Dance Theatre, founded in 1959 by a small group headed by an American teacher and choreographer, Ben Harkarvy. Harkarvy was joined as artistic director by a young Dutch choreographer, Hans van Manen. This company had the aim of using a combination of classical and modern dance techniques. This was not quite unprecedented (Yvonne Georgi, who directed one of the earlier attempts to plant a dance tradition in Holland, had tried something of the sort) but it was the first to aim successfully at the highest standard in both techniques.

John Butler (b. 1920)
Carmina Burana (Carl Orff) Netherlands Dance Theatre
Jaap Flier

Netherlands Dance Theatre started out with almost no resources except the unusual dedication of its members. Somehow they managed to keep together and build up both a repertory and an audience. By 1963 they were ready to venture abroad, making their first trips to Paris (for the Théâtre des Nations festival season) and to Britain. The most impressive features of the company at that time were the outstanding quality of the dancers and two ballets by American choreographers previously unknown in Europe. John Butler's *Carmina Burana* (to Carl Orff's rumbustious choral score, a kind of classical version of beat music) had originally been staged for the New York City Opera Company, but it suited the Dutch dancers as if it had been made for them. A passionate frenzy in its dances, relieved by quieter interludes, made it the company's meal ticket, more or less guaranteeing full houses whenever it was given. Glen Tetley's *Pierrot Lunaire* was an infinitely more subtle ballet, and even though it was one of his first works it illustrates the fascinating intellectual complexity of his approach, with its cross-references to *Petrushka* (written in the same year as Schoenberg's score), and its development of the old struggle—traditional since Roman days—between the white clown of innocence and the dark clown of experience. Yet although enriched by the underlying meanings that can be read into it, the ballet holds the imagination simply at surface value of its lively and often wrily amusing dance images.

A vital feature of Netherlands Dance Theatre was its sheer creativity. Every single work in the repertory was by a living choreographer. This is customary in modern dance companies, where the director is usually choreographer and leading dancer besides, but rare in ballet. Most of Dance Theatre's works were specially made for them, with an average of ten new ballets a year mounted consistently over the years, so that the dancers were constantly stimulated by new roles, but only the most successful works needed to be kept in the repertory. This formula proved so successful that before long other companies were copying it.

Carmina Burana Marianne Sarstädt

New stages, new audiences

I have mentioned so far, either at length or in passing, something like forty different companies. But for every one that attracts comment by virtue of some special merit or innovation, there are many more working away unnoticed. Just how many, I would not like even to estimate. The number is certainly large and has been increasing during the period under discussion.

In the Soviet Union alone, for instance, there are now at least thirty-six professional ballet companies, apart from amateur companies and others attached to operetta theatres. Several of these have appeared in the west: two from Moscow, two from Leningrad and one each from Kiev, Tbilisi and Novosibirsk. Dancers from others again have been seen as guest artists or in concert programmes—enough of them to make it clear that a pretty high standard is fairly general, but (as one would expect) by no means uniformly high. The Novosibirsk company is an example of one formed fairly recently to meet the needs of a developing neighbourhood; dancers were sent from elsewhere to start it off, including some promising soloists from the Kirov, and guest choreographers went to mount ballets for the initial repertory, although it was not long before the company developed its own resident choreographer, Oleg Vinogradov, who won a considerable reputation and was invited to work also in Moscow and Leningrad.

In America too the number of local companies has been steadily growing. The phenomenon known as 'regional ballet' has been gathering strength ever since it first crystallized at a regional ballet festival held in Atlanta, Georgia, in 1956. The term indicates a non-professional company (based usually on a dance school or even a group of schools) which regularly appears before paying audiences in works that are serious in intent even if sometimes limited in scope. The number of such companies runs into three figures; they serve to keep interest alive and sometimes to provide students with useful experience before starting a professional career. This kind of company seems primarily an American phenomenon, but there are a few instances of it elsewhere—even in Britain, where emphasis on regionalism in the arts has only just begun to flourish.

More recently a further kind of company has been helped to prosper in the United States by large grants from the Ford

Foundation (which also provided funds to ensure continuity for New York City Ballet and its associated School of American Ballet). There had long been professional companies of a long-term nature based outside New York: the San Francisco Ballet, for instance, which apart from any other virtues had produced many fine dancers who later graduated elsewhere. This and the more recently formed National Ballet (based in Washington) were among those to benefit, others being in Boston, Philadelphia and Utah. None of these has yet achieved anything remarkable in the creative sense; all of them so far rely heavily on revivals of works from the New York City Ballet's repertory—not only some of Balanchine's ballets, which is understandable, but one or two other less desirable acquisitions besides. On the other hand, they soon reached a reputable standard of performance which should make a good ground for further developments. Other local companies in the United States with a more than local standing include the Atlanta Ballet (which first encouraged David Blair to try the classical revivals at which he proved so successful) and a modern dance company in Salt Lake City with aid from the Rockefeller Foundation, which was given sufficient resources to invite distinguished choreographers to create works for its members.

All this is in addition to the various American touring companies based in New York. The longest established of these, American Ballet Theatre, was revived (after a period of disbandment forced on it by lack of funds) in time for a twenty-fifth anniversary

Bronislava Nijinska (b. 1891)
Les Noces (Stravinsky) The Royal Ballet
Svetlana Beriosova

season in 1964–5. Luckily this brought, among several new works and revivals, one creation of major importance to serve as a rallying force for the company's continuance. This was Stravinsky's *Les Noces*, staged by Jerome Robbins in accordance with the composer's original wishes with the singers, percussion players and pianists on stage. Bronislava Nijinska, in her production for Diaghilev (1923) had treated the ballet as a stylized version of Russian folk dances exactly parallel to Stravinsky's use of traditional Russian themes in his text and music. Robbins converted the ballet into a universal treatment of a marriage rite. Each version (Nijinska revived hers for the Royal Ballet in London the following year) was preferred to the other by some spectators—depending mainly on temperament, one imagines—but nobody denied that both had great power.

Ballet Theatre's twenty-fifth anniversary coincided with the debut of another major American company, the Harkness Ballet, founded by Rebekah Harkness, who had previously aided several other companies through the Foundation of which she was president. From the start her new company had fine dancers, but the repertory scarcely displayed them to great advantage. The best works in the early days were those inherited, together with several of the dancers, from one of Mrs Harkness' former beneficiaries, the Robert Joffrey Ballet. This company, originally founded by Joffrey on a small scale, grew over the years and had made many successful tours including one to Russia, but had to close down when it lost the Harkness backing on which it had come to rely. Fortunately a Ford Foundation grant made it possible for Joffrey to resume activity in 1965 after only one season's gap, and a successful season at New York City Center led to an invitation to be permanently associated with the Center and appear there regularly for several short seasons each year.

It becomes increasingly difficult to run a large-scale ballet company without some kind of financial support. In America this is generally provided by the big foundations or by tax-exempt endowments; in England and some British Commonwealth countries through the government-financed Arts Councils; elsewhere by municipal or state support. Luckily the prestige that can be won for a country or city by its arts helps to ensure that support will be forthcoming. Even countries with no previous tradition of ballet have started companies, and others have consolidated work

Pavel Smok (b. 1927)
Frescoes (Martinu) Ballet Prague

previously done sporadically by private enterprise. In this way Australia has formed a national ballet from the remnants of a former commercial company, Canada has endowed three major companies (in Montreal, Toronto and Winnipeg), New Zealand also has a company and the four provinces of South Africa each have one.

It might be expected that support of this sort would discourage experiment, but this does not prove to be the case. Indeed, there are examples of 'official' companies specifically started for the sake of experiment—the Sopiane Ballet at Pecs in Hungary, the Ballet

Prague with its base in the subsidized Theatre Studio, the Leningrad Chamber Ballet directed by the esteemed veteran choreographer and teacher Pyotr Gusev and the Young Ballet Company founded in Moscow by Igor Moiseyev. In France a company (Ballet Théâtre Contemporain) devoted entirely to new work, and specifically to twentieth-century music as the basis of all its ballets, was founded recently in the Maison de la Culture at Amiens; and the choreographer Joseph Lazzini, whose period as director of ballet in the municipal opera house at Marseilles was marked by much iconoclastic experiment, is at the time of writing about to form a new company on behalf of the Ministry of Culture to be known as Théâtre Français de la Danse. The *maisons de la*

Pavel Smok
Gangrene (Charlie Mingus) Ballet Prague

Joseph Lazzini (b. 1927)
Le Fils Prodigue (Prokofiev) Marseilles Municipal Ballet
Jean Babilée

culture established throughout France as centres for the arts are one example of the deliberate expansion of provision to enable wider sections of the public to share what was formerly a minority privilege. They are built and maintained with state funds; in America, where similar projects were planned, the need to rely mainly on private patronage or charitable trusts has meant a slower start except for the ambitious Lincoln Center in New York with its State Theater (planned primarily as a dance theatre to Balanchine's requirements) and its rebuilt Metropolitan Opera House, frequently used for visiting dance companies.

At the other extreme, artists without official backing have found ingenious ways to present their work. In New York a church in Judson Square became a home for avant-garde dance experiments; in London an old building near Covent Garden was converted at negligible cost into an 'arts laboratory'. Small groups of dancers have found it possible to tour towns without a theatre large enough for a full-scale company, appearing sometimes in school halls or other makeshift substitutes for a proper theatre.

The obvious opportunities for bringing ballet to the greatest possible number of people, television and film, have remained comparatively little developed. Although the few feature films that have been made (usually of stage ballets performed by famous stars, and either photographed straight or adapted in only the most perfunctory way) are shown repeatedly on the art cinema circuits, no really successful film has yet been made of a ballet specifically designed for the screen. In television, there have been some useful experiments. Alwin Nikolais in New York, whose Dance Theatre relies on unusual costumes, lighting and stage effects, has prepared works specially for television incorporating ideas that would only be feasible in that medium with the aid of multiple cameras and electronic devices. Peter Darrell, in two ballets specially created with Western Theatre Ballet for BBC television, explored the idea that ordinary dancing on the small screen always looks out of place and that what was really needed was simple movement based on a dancer's sense of rhythm and timing rather than any defined technique. His subjects in *Houseparty* (an original treatment of Poulenc's music for *Les Biches*) and *Orpheus* (with the

Peter Darrell
A Man Like Orpheus (Raymond Leppard) Western Theatre Ballet for *BBC* Television
Suzanne Hywel, Peter Cazalet

hero seen as a pop star and Eurydice as a beautiful model girl) were too esoteric for mass appeal, but the works themselves— both with plots by a playwright, John Hopkins—were far from negligible. Considering how many more people can see ballet on film or television than on stage, it seems astonishing that the problems of translating it into the different media have met with little attention and even less success. A few producers (often former dancers, like Margaret Dale of the BBC) have found ways of effecting a reasonable compromise to show stage ballets on the screen; these are likely to become more satisfactory as the use of colour television becomes general. But there is a vast field still open for the person who evolves ways of creating works satisfactorily from scratch for the large or small screen. Even when this is achieved, it will be a supplement rather than a rival to live performances with their immediacy of contact between the performer and the spectator, but this limitation still leaves it worth trying.

Meanwhile, ballet on stage goes on finding new and larger audiences. Apart from the examples previously mentioned, the most striking instance of expansion lately has been in Germany, not formerly much noted for an interest in ballet. But any town of any size at all had its municipal theatre, and after the war ballet companies sprang up in many of them. Often they had British or American directors, drawing on the experience of these countries in the same way that these had formerly drawn on that of the Russians. Most of the German companies were modest in their aims and achievements, but some began to become more prominent than others, and one of them quite conspicuously so. This was the company of the Württemberg State Theatres at Stuttgart, where the South African John Cranko (formerly a resident

Kenneth MacMillan
Das Lied von der Erde (Mahler) Württemberg State Ballet, Stuttgart
Marcia Haydee, Ray Barra, Egon Madsen

choreographer at Sadler's Wells and Covent Garden) had been director since 1961. At first Cranko attracted famous stars to work with his company, including Fonteyn, Bruhn and Nureyev, but his aim was to build a true ensemble. By 1963 the company was strong enough to take part in the Edinburgh International Festival, and two years later, on 7 November 1965, the Stuttgart stage saw the double première of two works specially created for the company which have since been recognized as masterpieces. One was Kenneth MacMillan's *Das Lied von der Erde*, to Mahler's mighty score for singers and orchestra. MacMillan had wanted to produce this for the Royal Ballet but the Covent Garden direction thought the music unsuitable. After its success in Stuttgart, it was eagerly admitted after all to the Royal Ballet repertory. The other new work that night, Cranko's *Opus I* to music by Webern, had the same theme as *Das Lied von der Erde* : man's brief life, the inevitability of death but the continuance of life itself. MacMillan treated it on a

Das Lied von der Erde Egon Madsen, Marcia Haydee

huge scale, Cranko as a miniature. Both ballets were original, powerful, poetic and moving.

Opus I represented one side of Cranko's talent: the urge to do something new. His experimental ballets in Stuttgart have included one inspired by the paintings of Francis Bacon, *The Interrogation*, and one to music by the avant-garde composer Bernd Alois Zimmermann, *Présence*, in which the three leading characters are archetypal figures from literature, Molly Bloom, Don Quixote and Ubu Roi, representing different aspects of man's nature, sexual, idealistic and earthily opportunist. *Présence* is unusual not only in theme but in presentation too, with explicit mimed passages interspersed with enigmatic passages of dancing. Yet Cranko is also a traditionalist, having mounted for his company a series of large-scale narrative ballets including *Romeo and Juliet*, *Swan Lake* (in a completely new version with a genuinely tragic ending—the wicked magician triumphant, the prince

John Cranko
Onegin (Tchaikovsky) Württemburg State Ballet, Stuttgart
Marcia Haydee, Ray Barra

The Taming of the Shrew Marcia Haydee, Richard Cragun

John Cranko
The Taming of the Shrew (music Kurt-Heinz Stolze based on Scarlatti)
Württemburg State Ballet, Stuttgart
Egon Madsen, Susanne Hanke

drowned and Odette still transformed into a swan), *Onegin* and *The Taming of the Shrew*. More perhaps than any choreographer today, Cranko is a master story-teller, but he tells his stories entirely in dancing. Through these works he has developed the artistry of his dancers until his Brazilian-born ballerina Marcia Haydee is now one of the finest dancers anywhere in the world, equally great in tragedy (as Juliet or Tatiana) or in comedy (as Kate in *The Shrew*).

Among the other German companies, only one has come near to rivalling Cranko's achievements, namely the Ballet of the Deutsche Oper, Berlin, during the three years since Kenneth MacMillan went there as director in 1966. MacMillan also presented a mixture of big-scale traditional works and others of a more advanced nature. His best work in the one type was a production of *The Sleeping Beauty* largely following Petipa's brilliant classical choreography but designed with almost unprecedented splendour (and cost) by Barry Kay. On the other hand MacMillan mounted *Anastasia*, a dramatic exploration of the mind of the woman who claimed to be the surviving member of the Russian imperial family. With Lynn Seymour as the heroine, this ballet used a soundtrack as well as music, incorporated films as part of its action and crowded a nightmare realism into its formalized action. But although under MacMillan's direction the Berlin company became internationally famous in the same way that Stuttgart had done under Cranko, the theatre authorities gave the ballet little priority in terms of performing time or opportunity for new productions, and in the summer of 1969 MacMillan left. It seemed likely that, with Balanchine as guest choreographer, some prestige would remain for the company, but not the impetus that can come only from a full-time creative director. In this respect Berlin resigned precedence to Stuttgart, where the only factor inhibiting further development is the restriction on the number of performances imposed by the presence also of opera and drama companies. There has been much discussion, however, of the possibility of amalgamating with a ballet company from another city to provide what would be more like a national company (which in standards, although not in material conditions, the Stuttgart Ballet already is). A possible step towards bringing about this hope was Cranko's recent acceptance of responsibility also for productions at Munich. If this succeeds, his already impressive achievements may be redoubled.

New men, new methods

The changes in ballet which we have noted so far sprang mainly from influences within the art itself by a process of cross-fertilization. But no art exists in a vacuum, and ballet has been equally changed by new ideas in the other arts or in society as a whole. Think of the clothes people wore, the books they read, movies they watched and music they listened to perhaps ten years ago; all have changed and so, in the same way, has ballet. The biggest change of all has been the discovery of a new way of conveying meaning. Once a film would have needed to explain who its characters were, where they were and why; now directors leave more to the imagination. The 'new novel' sees no need to explain itself either. Even a necessarily simple art like pop music can use lyrics which would have seemed incomprehensible to a previous generation, and the theatre shows the same tendency, to the point where the authors of *Hair* asked Tom Horgan, when he directed it, to cut out the spoken dialogue as far as possible to make it as little like a conventional musical as could be. Yet *Hair* did not end up really without a plot; it merely conveyed the situation and its development by the music, lyrics and stage action without need for any

Gerald Arpino *Clowns* (Hershy Kay) City Center Joffrey Ballet
Robert Blankshine

Clowns Robert Blankshine
also opposite

explicit story-line. Increasingly it is becoming true, if not that 'the medium is the message', at least that the message of any work of art can be expressed only in its own medium. Marshal McLuhan's theories merely crystallize what people were already thinking.

In ballet the change came about mainly at first within the companies which were following the lead of Netherlands Dance Theatre towards a mixture of classical and modern dancing. Possibly the breaking down of one barrier encouraged revolutionary thoughts, or perhaps it was merely that these companies attracted many of the most intelligent and forward-looking artists.

One of these companies is the City Center Joffrey Ballet in New York. Although Joffrey astutely mixes into his programmes some older works which he thinks will entertain and add variety, the company relies largely on works created for it, mainly by the resident choreographer Gerald Arpino. These range from the exuberant *Viva Vivaldi!*—a display piece which became almost the company's signature work—through *Olympics*, designed to show off the male dancers, to the mysterious *Nightwings* (a strange, nightmarish piece) and *Clowns*, which uses those generally amiable beings as the characters for an allegory of man destroying himself through war.

Joffrey himself, however, was the choreographer of *Astarte*, a multi-media work of deliberately sensational qualities. To music by a raga-rock group, the Crome Syrkus, and amid a bombardment of lights, the male dancer left a seat in the stalls, went on stage, stripped to his briefs and danced an erotic duet with the girl he found there, while filmed images of them on a screen behind dwarfed them both. At the end he walked away under the back-cloth and the film showed the supposed continuation of his journey, leaving the back of the theatre through the car park still in his near-naked state which attracted no attention at all. The ballet, with its fierce assault on the senses through loud music and blinding lights, its unexplained but compelling images and its creation of a mood related to current pop art and drug experimentation, was a great hit and contributed to establishing the company as a vital feature of the New York theatrical scene. Its qualities were typical of the new spirit coming into ballet.

In Britain the old-established Ballet Rambert was affected by the changes. The exigencies of touring had obliged it (because provincial managements insisted that audiences wanted only works they had heard of) to rely mainly on a few classic revivals, to which its mainly young dancers were not always well suited, at the expense of the repertory of creations by all leading British choreographers which it had built up over three decades. Finally in 1966 the increased costs of touring a large orchestra and corps de ballet forced a crisis. The company had to change or go out of business. Norman Morrice, a dancer in the company, who since his choreographic debut eight years earlier had made one work a year for the company (all the experimentation it could afford), was made associate director and largely allowed to plan the new developments, which he modelled closely on Netherlands Dance Theatre. His own ballets had always shown a strong involvement with real life, including an attack on authoritarianism in *The Travellers* and a study of the way dancers' own lives and their work react upon each other in *Conflicts*. Gradually he brought the always interesting content of his ballets under greater formal control, as in the recent lyrical *Pastorale Variée* and also in *1-2-3*

Norman Morrice (b. 1931)
1-2-3 (Ben-Zim Orgad) Ballet Rambert
Mary Willis, Christopher Bruce, Bob Smith

(created originally for the Batsheva Dance Company in Israel), a work of sculptural beauty and musical sensitivity about the birth of man and his doomed struggle for love.

Besides his own works, however, Morrice was keen to encourage new choreographers. John Chesworth, another of the leading dancers, soon emerged as a producer of remarkably original ideas and theatrical flair. In 'H' he produced an effective manifesto in movement about the H-bomb, and in *Pawn to King 5* (to music by

John Chesworth (b. 1930)
Pawn to King 5 (The Pink Floyd) Ballet Rambert
Gideon Avrahami, Sandra Craig

Norman Morrice *Pastorale Variée* (Paul Ben-Haim) Ballet Rambert

a pop group, The Pink Floyd) a remarkable essay on violence in society and its infectious nature, expressed in a series of images drawn from discothèque dancing, a portrait of a wounded soldier and a Japanese Kabuki-style ritual suicide. In addition, Ballet

Amanda Knott (b. 1945)
Curiouser and Curiouser (Elliot Carter) Ballet Rambert/Collaboration 2
Peter Curtis

Rambert started a series of 'Collaboration' programmes involving students from art and music colleges in the creation of new works by aspiring choreographers, mainly—but not exclusively—from within the company.

Clover Roope (b. 1939)
Solo (Alexander Goehr) Ballet Rambert/Collaboration 2
Christopher Bruce

Rambert also proved, in its new incarnation, one of several homes for the rapidly developing talent of Glen Tetley, who had by now left Netherlands Dance Theatre although he continued to mount ballets for them as well as for Rambert, for the Batsheva Company in Tel Aviv, for the new University of Utah modern dance company in Salt Lake City, for American Ballet Theatre and for his own touring company. This strenuous round of activity, far from exhausting his inspiration, seemed to fire it afresh. Tetley's early ballets, although always expressed in dance images rather than explicit acting, had contained a clear theme: man as victim, destroyer and discoverer in *The Anatomy Lesson*, woman

The Anatomy Lesson Jaap Flier

Glen Tetley
The Anatomy Lesson (Marcel Landowski) Netherlands Dance Theatre

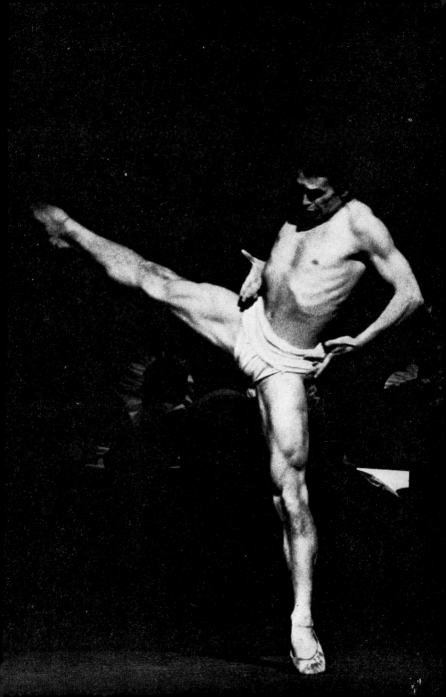

becalmed in unhappy middle age in *Sargasso*. Now he began to refine away content to an extent that it could be understood by the spectator but not easily or exactly put into words. In *Mythical Hunters* the content of the dances is images of hunting, flight and capture; this becomes a metaphor for the relationship of man and woman and also (by a process whereby each captured prey gives birth to a successor) an image of the generations.

Glen Tetley
Sargasso (Ernst Krenek) Netherlands Dance Theatre
Nils Christe, Willy de la Bije

Glen Tetley
Mythical Hunters (Oedoen Partos) Netherlands Dance Theatre

Mythical Hunters Marianne Sarstädt, Gérard Lemaitre

Freefall explores almost all the ideas that title could suggest: not only the physical act of falling (although that recurs throughout the ballet) but the idea of breaking loose from all conventional

Glen Tetley
Freefall (Max Schubel) Ballet Rambert
Sandra Craig, Christopher Bruce, Gayrie MacSween

restraints and attachments. With duets of a ferociously sexual
nature not only for men with women, but man with man and
woman with woman, the work digs into human nature for some

underlying needs or desires. Sometimes Tetley's inspiration is musical, as in *Circles* to Berio's score: sometimes drawn from visual art, as in *Ziggurat* where he develops themes taken from ancient Assyrian art; and sometimes physical—*Embrace Tiger and Return to Mountain* started with study of a book of instruction in the Chinese exercises of T'ai-chi, one of which provides the title.

Circles Willy de la Bije, Jaap Flier

Glen Tetley
Circles (Luciano Berio) Netherlands Dance Theatre

Glen Tetley
Embrace Tiger and Return to Mountain (Morton Subotnick) Ballet Rambert
Mary Willis
also opposite

Embrace Tiger and Return to Mountain Mary Willis, Christopher Bruce

The great advantage of the free-structured, associative form Tetley prefers is that it can communicate on different levels simultaneously. He likes to explore round the edges of an idea, following a situation through time and also catching other peripheral subjects on the way. In one of his latest ballets, *Arena*, the setting is clearly contemporary (a changing-room where athletes fight out their own contests of personality) but the pink-painted bodies of the minimally-clad men bring to mind the bull-dancers of ancient Crete.

Because of the large number of companies he has worked for and the many different countries in which his work has been seen, Tetley has had a wide influence. On the other hand, what he is doing is not unique but his own development (rather more intensive than most) of lines on which others have worked.

on pages 120 and 121
Christopher Bruce (b. 1945)
George Frideric (Handel) Ballet Rambert
Gayrie MacSween

Glen Tetley
Arena (Morton Subotnick) Netherlands Dance Theatre
Frans Vervenne, Jaap Flier

Merce Cunningham's *Place*, for instance, could scarcely be defined in literary terms. Some kind of struggle for territory is clearly going on : a man carefully tends his own little space, but in the end undergoes defeat, which leads him to clamber into a large plastic bag that covers him completely as he rolls away out of sight at the back. That much is clear, and it is all the audience needs to know ; the sense of despair, struggle and defeat communicates itself directly without any need for a story.

Similarly with Paul Taylor's ambitious *Orbs*, which manages to catch the splendour of Beethoven's late string quartets in dance. Even though this contains episodes which can be clearly defined— the sun teaching the planets how to make love ; a comic wedding in which the sun is transformed into a tipsy, bottom-pinching priest—their significance and relationship make sense at an instinctive rather than an intellectual level. Narrate this ballet and it would sound silly ; dance it and it becomes a hymn in praise of man in his elements.

Merce Cunningham
Place (Gordon Mumma) Merce Cunningham Dance Company
Cunningham

Paul Taylor
Orbs (Beethoven) Paul Taylor Dance Company

The latest generation of choreographers have grown up in the atmosphere of new discoveries and turn naturally to work that exploits their freedom to do things their own way. One of the most striking examples is Hans van Manen, who developed entirely within Netherlands Dance Theatre. Starting as an admirer of Balanchine, Robbins and Roland Petit, he found his own voice by experiment. In each ballet he set himself a difficulty to overcome, a special form to follow, for instance in *Metaphors* where he based all the movements on mirror-images, but managed to convey fresh ideas of what emotional and intellectual content should be read into dance patterns. In *Five Sketches* he tried to emphasize the effort that goes into dancing, which dancers usually try to hide; in the process he created a fresh, Eden-like mood with a bitter ending. A particularly fine and original work is his *Solo for Voice 1*, to John Cage's music of the same name, in which he put the singer on stage with the dancers and used her as a figure seeming to inspire, incite and provoke the two dancers who were

Hans van Manen (b. 1932)
Five Sketches (Hindemith) Netherlands Dance Theatre
Han Ebbelar, Alexandra Radius

Hans van Manen
Solo for Voice 1 (John Cage) Netherlands Dance Theatre
Anne Haenen, Susan Kenniff, Hans Knill

made to appear completely occupied with themselves all the time in a kind of cool mating ritual.

It was a logical consequence of the experiments taking place in the form and content of ballet that the kind of music used and the visual design of costumes and setting should also change. Traditional melodies and conventional frilled dresses are not likely to suit ballets that aim seriously to say something about life today. Merce Cunningham has particularly been a pioneer so far as music is concerned : the first presentation of *musique concrète* in the United States was his solo, *Collage*, to an extract from Pierre Schaeffer's Symphonie pour un Homme Seul, and his *Suite by Chance* was the first dance work with a pure electronic sound score, commissioned from Christian Wolff. His collaboration with John Cage has been consistent and close. This makes some of his work difficult for an uninitiated audience to accept—even when Cage is in his most benign mood, such as the 'score' for *How to Pass, Kick, Fall and Run* which consists of the composer sitting at the side of the stage and reading highly entertaining extracts from one of his books to a stop-watch timing.

But although the use of modern music sometimes makes life harder for the choreographers and dancers, it is observable that even the most difficult music becomes easier to follow when it is accompanied by relevant movement. And the music for its part can lead the choreographer into paths he might not otherwise have found—as, for instance, in Jaap Flier's *Nouvelles Aventures* to music by György Ligeti, where the dancers explore a kind of limbo of the soul before finding themselves squashed ignominiously by the droppings of the gods.

The musical policy of the more experimental companies is such that works like Schoenberg's *Pierrot Lunaire* (long admired as a landmark of modern music, but seldom played) are now regularly heard, and that the work of contemporary composers however advanced is likely to get a hearing. One interesting development, incidentally, is the increasing use of vocal music (usually with an orchestral accompaniment) as a basis for ballet, a mixture that can be rewarding and could well be adapted to a closer collaboration with singers in future.

Jaap Flier (b. 1934)
Nouvelles Aventures (György Ligeti) Netherlands Dance Theatre
Lenny Westerdijk

Alwin Nikolais (b. 1912)
Tent (Nikolais) Alwin Nikolais Dance Theatre

Alwin Nikolais
Somniloquy (Nikolais) Alwin Nikolais Dance Theatre

Design for ballet has changed in a way very like the accompanying music, although partly for different reasons. An economic factor affecting the issue is that music, generally speaking, is an essential, but ballet can be danced in the simplest costumes with no decor. Sometimes this is a positive advantage; Balanchine's ballets, for instance, often look best in practice clothes (tights and leotard or singlet). At the other extreme has been what seemed a contest between designers to achieve the most grandiose naturalistic setting for a classic revival. In general, however, the tendency has been towards simplicity and solidity. Martha Graham pioneered the use of sculpture in the designing of ballets and this has proved remarkably successful. Screens, cut-outs, projections, scaffolding and other objects have become more common; realistic painted backcloths less so. Texture, colour and shape are the qualities that

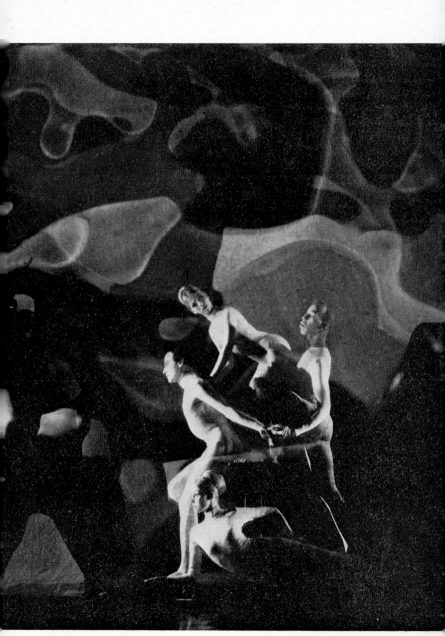

matter. The aim is to provide an environment for the dance rather than a moving picture. In costume the changes have been equally striking. Sometimes they are imaginative to an almost outrageous degree, but in general the clothes dancers wear in modern works have tended to become more like those they wear off-stage. There are companies that use classical technique but do not have a single tutu in the wardrobe.

Also, as designs became simpler, lighting grew more ambitious. Jean Rosenthal in America first introduced effects with low side lighting picking out the individual dancers from surrounding darkness; others branching out from her discoveries have made

stage lighting an art of its own. Revealingly, when Rauschenberg was artistic director for Cunningham one of the things he took great care of was the lighting, rather than more obvious aspects.

That design and lighting could become almost a primary art in themselves is shown by the Alwin Nikolais Dance Theatre of New York. Nikolais who is choreographer, designer and composer for his own works, often conceals his dancers wholly or partly in costumes that completely hide the shape of the body, and uses tricks of lighting (with unusual colours, or alternating areas of light and darkness so that a dancer can seem to appear and disappear) as an integral part of his programmes.

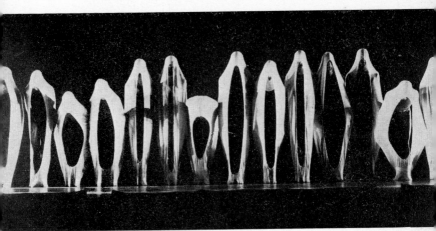

Alwin Nikolais
Sanctum (Nikolais) Alwin Nikolais Dance Theatre
also opposite

In design, as in other respects, the experimentation of some companies has forced changes even upon those which cling to a traditional policy. Thus the Royal Ballet, for instance, has used pop-art designs (for *Jazz Calendar*, which also used composed jazz music) and psychedelic lighting effects (in *Sinfonietta*). The effect of this sort of thing is only skin deep, but it does seem also that the Royal Ballet has been more deeply affected by the changes taking place around it. During the period since Frederick Ashton became director in 1963 the repertory has become more adventurous. Two of his own creations have been especially noteworthy: *Monotones* in which he used the simplest possible means —two trios of dancers, starkly simple costumes, Satie music and a bare stage—to create a ballet of limpid beauty; and *Enigma Variations* in which he transformed what could have been an embarrassingly fulsome parade of characters by concentrating on the noblest aspect of Elgar's music and creating to it a unique expression in dancing of the quality of friendship. In addition, Ashton invited his old colleague Antony Tudor back from America to revive his poignant pre-war *Jardin aux Lilas* (about a girl trying to say goodbye to her lover before a marriage of convenience) and to create two new works. One of these, *Shadowplay*, used an unlikely combination of a situation from Kipling's *Jungle Book*, a treatment from oriental sources and modern French music for a calm, quiet allegory of a boy growing up; the other, *Knight Errant*, was a very explicit bawdy comedy based on *Les Liaisons Dangereuses*.

Frederick Ashton
Enigma Variations (Elgar) The Royal Ballet
Svetlana Beriosova, Derek Rencher

Antony Tudor (b. 1909)
Jardin aux Lilas (Chausson) The Royal Ballet
Antoinette Sibley, Ronald Hynd

Jardin aux Lilas Antoinette Sibley, Anthony Dowell

Ashton's flair as director was for concentrating on what his dancers were best suited to, and selecting from current fashions only what could be absorbed into their work without detriment to its enduring qualities. Similarly in New York, Balanchine largely went his own way although venturing from time to time into regions of more complex modern music such as the scores by Yannis Xenakis he used for *Metastaseis & Pithoprakta*. Concurrently, however, he was also presenting ballets like his full-evening *Don Quixote* to some undistinguished music specially written by Nicolas Nabokov, and a new version of *Harlequinade* to music by the unfashionable Drigo (one of Petipa's regular composers). One surprising creation was the first full-evening

George Balanchine
Harlequinade (Drigo) New York City Ballet
Edward Villella

Antony Tudor
Shadowplay (Charles Koechlin) The Royal Ballet
Anthony Dowell

Eliot Feld (b. 1942)
Harbinger (Prokofiev) American Ballet Theatre

Eliot Feld
At Midnight (Mahler) American Ballet Theatre
Bruce Marks

plotless ballet, *Jewels*, but this was danced to three independent pieces of music by Fauré, Stravinsky and Tchaikovsky. In 1969 Jerome Robbins was persuaded to renew his former connexion with New York City Ballet and created for them *Dances at a Gathering*, a work lasting more than an hour to Chopin piano music, with no plot, but evoking ideas of a lost European past.

Companies without an Ashton or Balanchine, Robbins or Tudor to call upon either had to find new talent or borrow talent from elsewhere. American Ballet Theatre were fortunate in developing a new choreographer within the company, Eliot Feld. His *Harbinger*, a pure dance work, marked an auspiciously individual debut; *At Midnight* (to four of Mahler's five Ruckert songs) followed this with an individual expression of the lightness and the despair of love—the latter quality predominating.

Choreographers of quality are rare, but without them a company either stagnates or falls into triviality. A case in point was the Royal Danish Ballet which, after free-wheeling for years on the strength of its inherited Bournonville repertory, was losing its impetus and dancing even these classics less well than it should. Under a new director, Flemming Flindt, who took over in 1965, the company became livelier again. New productions of some of the Bournonville ballets were mounted, and Flindt himself produced a number of new works, including a vigorously brawling *Three Musketeers* and a rather abstract treatment of Bartók's *Miraculous Mandarin*. Unfortunately none of Flindt's later works recaptured the dramatic power of his first ballet, a gripping adaptation into

on pages 142 *and* 143
Flemming Flindt
The Miraculous Mandarin (Bartók) Royal Danish Ballet
Flindt, Vivi Gelker

Flemming Flindt (b. 1936)
The Three Musketeers (Georges Delerue) Royal Danish Ballet
Henning Kronstam, Kirsten Simone

balletic terms of Ionesco's play, *The Private Lesson*, about an apparently mild teacher who kills his pupil when carried away by the power he acquires over her. However, Flindt also brought into the repertory some unexpected works by American choreographers. First came Jerome Robbins' *Afternoon of a Faun*, using the same music as Nijinsky's famous ballet but presenting the idea in terms of narcissistic dancers in a studio instead of the original mythological faun and nymphs. Later two modern dance works were added, Paul Taylor's *Aureole* and Glen Tetley's *Pierrot Lunaire*. By enlarging the scope of the dancers, these did much to put fresh spirit into the company.

Flemming Flindt
The Lesson (Georges Delerue) Western Theatre Ballet
Simon Mottram, Arlette van Boven

Jerome Robbins
Afternoon of a Faun (Debussy) Royal Danish Ballet
Henning Kronstam, Kirsten Simone

Flindt is only one of many young men who have lately taken charge of companies, either long established or recent foundations. The Bolshoi Ballet is now directed by Yuri Grigorovich, who in one of his latest works for them, *Spartacus*, has repeated the achievement of his first work, *The Stone Flower*, in making a success of a ballet formerly unsuccessful, again by treating in terms of dancing what had previously been the subject of heavy acting. Kenneth MacMillan and John Field (the latter a dancer turned director who has for some years run the Royal Ballet's touring company) are about to take over the direction of the Royal Ballet from Ashton; and Lawrence Rhodes, the brilliant (and intelligent) young leading dancer of the Harkness Ballet, recently became

opposite
Yuri Grigorovich
Spartacus (Khachaturian) Bolshoi Ballet
Vladimir Vasiliev

Spartacus Boris Akimov

director of that company. Not being himself a choreographer, he invited several outsiders to create or revive works for the company, with an immediately beneficial effect on the previously uninspired repertory. In Holland, too, the large and well-endowed National Ballet, which always presented a curious appearance of artistic split personality, has begun to look like a more serious rival to Netherlands Dance Theatre since the young choreographer Rudi van Dantzig became director lately. He has a fine gift for using classical technique in an original way. *Monument for a Dead Boy*, his most famous work, vividly and compassionately expresses in flashback the life of a boy who died young: his squalid home background, his aspirations, his loves (both hetero- and homo-sexual) and his artistic gifts. Unfortunately works like this, or an impressive revival of Kurt Jooss' anti-war ballet of the 1930s, *The Green Table*, were swamped in an enormous repertory of variable quality. Under van Dantzig's leadership it seems likely that may change.

Rudi van Dantzig (b. 1933)
Monument for a Dead Boy (Jan Boerman) Netherlands National Ballet
Rudolf Nureyev

Kurt Jooss (b. 1901)
The Green Table (Fritz Cohen) Netherlands National Ballet

A completely new company, American Dance Players, is at the time of writing being formed by Eliot Feld, who left Ballet Theatre to become a freelance choreographer. In Britain also a new company is being prepared by Laverne Meyer (formerly associate artistic director of Western Theatre Ballet) to be based on Manchester—evidence of a new emphasis on ballet outside London, underlined by the fact that Western Theatre Ballet itself has changed both its name and its home, becoming Scottish Theatre Ballet in association with Scottish Opera in Glasgow. In addition, the London Contemporary Dance Company, after a couple of years of very limited activity (one trial week of the full company outside London, several choreographic workshops and tours by a lecture-demonstration group) is preparing its first proper season. The aim of the company has always been, while importing the Graham technique, to find new choreographers of its own, and already one of its dancers, Barry Moreland, has shown much promise in his *Summer Games*, a happily nostalgic evocation of youthful summers. But things move so fast now in the world of dance that by the time this book appears these events will be history.

on pages 152 *and* 153
Geoff Moore (b. 1944)
Remembered Motion (Malcolm Fox) Ballet Rambert
Nicoline Nystrom, Peter Curtis

Barry Moreland (b. 1942)
Summer Games (Samuel Barber) London Contemporary Dance Company
Clare Duncan, Barry Moreland

This account is almost finished, but the story is by no means over. With so many new men in charge, ballet is bound to go on changing. And the increasing popularity of the new trends I have outlined, especially among young people with some background in music, painting and sculpture, should ensure that their development continues. There is, besides, a growing tendency for young painters and sculptors to concern themselves actively in the production or performance of events involving dance. In New York it has happened for some time, in London it is becoming more usual. One such young painter, Geoff Moore, has already formed his own multi-media group, Moving Being, for the presentation of works involving several techniques but with movement predominant, and his first programmes have been encouragingly successful.

Ballet has become a far more serious art over these past few years, but thank goodness it has not become a solemn one. People who watch it regularly are likely to find themselves often both surprised and delighted. Whatever else happens to it in future, it seems likely to remain lively and unpredictable.

George Balanchine
Episodes (Webern) New York City Ballet
Patricia Neary

Index

Photo credits

BBC 90; Connoisseur Films 8, 10; Anthony Crickmay 29, 35, 53, 56–7, 61, 82, 83, 96, 103, 105, 108, 109, 114, 115, 124, 127, 144; Frederica Davis 47, 58; Gala Films 15; Grands Ballets Canadiens 17; Bob Johnson 59; Hannes Kilian 97; Serge Lido 44, 89; A. Makarov 146, 147; Particam 22, 23, 123; Houston Rogers 49; Roy Round 54, 55; Werner Schloske 94, 95; Lord Snowdon 31; Alo Storz 93; Hans van den Busken 148; Mogens van Haven 52, 74, 75, 141, 145; Jennie Walton 37, 122; Victor Welsh 71; Rosemary Winckley front cover, 12, 13, 20, 21, 24, 25, 32, 36, 48, 50, 51, 77, 78, 80, 81, 104, 106, 107, 110, 111, 112, 113, 116, 117, 118, 119, 120–21, 125, 132, 134, 135, 142–3, 151, 152–3.

STUDIO VISTA/DUTTON PICTUREBACKS

edited by David Herbert

British churches by Edwin Smith and Olive Cook
European domestic architecture by Sherban Cantacuzino
Great modern architecture by Sherban Cantacuzino
Modern churches of the world
by Robert Maguire and Keith Murray
Modern houses of the world by Sherban Cantacuzino

African sculpture by William Fagg and Margaret Plass
European sculpture by David Bindman
Florentine sculpture by Anthony Bertram
Greek sculpture by John Barron
Indian sculpture by Philip Rawson
Michelangelo by Anthony Bertram
Modern sculpture by Alan Bowness

Art deco by Bevis Hillier
Art nouveau by Mario Amaya
The bauhaus by Gillian Naylor
De Stijl by Paul Overy
Modern graphics by Keith Murgatroyd
Modern prints by Pat Gilmour
Pop art: object and image by Christopher Finch
Surrealism by Robert Stuart Short and Roger Cardinal
1000 years of drawing by Anthony Bertram

Arms and armour by Howard L. Blackmore
The art of the garden by Miles Hadfield
Art in silver and gold by Gerald Taylor
Costume in pictures by Phillis Cunnington
Firearms by Howard L. Blackmore
Jewelry by Graham Hughes
Modern ballet by John Percival
Modern ceramics by Geoffrey Beard
Modern furniture by Ella Moody
Modern glass by Geoffrey Beard
Motoring history by L. T. C. Rolt
Railway history by C. Hamilton Ellis
Toys by Patrick Murray

Charlie Chaplin: early comedies by Isabel Quigly
The films of Alfred Hitchcock by George Perry
The great funnies by David Robinson
Greta Garbo by Raymond Durgnat and John Kobal
Marlene Dietrich by John Kobal
Movie monsters by Denis Gifford
New cinema in Britain by Roger Manvell
New cinema in Europe by Roger Manvell
New cinema in the USA by Roger Manvell
The silent cinema by Liam O'Leary